RATTLED AWAKE

Volume One

Anthology Series

CONTENTS

ACKNOWLEDGEMENTS

I, Lonnee Rey, owe a debt of gratitude to Mark O'Brien, who immediately saw my vision for *Rattled Awake*, and ran with it. From day one, his "we got this kid" attitude and actions epitomized the expression, "There is no 'I' in team." His cheerful outlook propped me up on a personal level, acting as self-assigned head cheerleader and faith-builder.

His out-of-character promotional efforts were done because, as he said, "It's just the right thing to do."

Mark created opportunities to present Rattled Awake to his writing group, and enrolled his personal network, including the illustrious Dennis Pitocco, to help spread the word. What an honor it is to have these men standing in support of the long-reaching vision, and impactful series, this is destined to become.

Mark's grasp of the vision for *Rattled Awake* prompted him to connect with people working in the fields of domestic violence and abuse, with intentional focus on creating a future volume…one that will give voice to those who don't yet have one.

Blessings come when we step off the curb and move forward. Mark O'Brien has been that blessing, a priceless gift and a true friend; one whose help has brought forth this flagship book in a series that will change lives, just as he has done for me, for us, and for those whose lives will be positively influenced by these stories.

INTRODUCTION

These are just a few of the comments the authors expressed while writing their chapter in one weekend.

"I suck at writing."
"I'm told I'm a good writer but I have no
idea how to start my own story."
"I can't believe I did it! In school, my English
teacher called me a lunk."
"I consider myself a good writer, but this
was really challenging to me."

And yet, they did it...never underestimate yourself and the power of commitment, coaching and collaboration!

"Rattled Awake" was born out of the idea that we have all been 'shaken' and changed – how to become better, not bitter, in response. It was created with you in mind.

Whether a first time or experienced writer, each rose to challenge in answering, "Over the past five years, what is the single most significant event that rattled you awake?" Who have you become as a result? These are their stories.

CONTRIBUTORS

Dreams came to life thanks to these incredibly dedicated writers and visionaries.

It truly would not be the same without you, the amazing co-authors of the #1 International Best Selling book, "Rattled Awake"

Chef Jill Sullivan
Chris Freer
Erika Warfield
LeeAnna Stock-Luoma
Susannah Dawn
Dr. Constance Leyland
Nicole Angai-Galindo
Russ Hedge
Willie J.
Lonnee Rey
Steve Kidd

YOU'RE NEVER TOO OLD TO REWRITE YOUR NEXT CHAPTER ~CHEF JILL SULLIVAN

You're never too old to rewrite your next chapter and change-up your script

My life was turned upside down in 2004 when my husband Marc and I decided to leave Hemet, California, to pursue a new life in Utah. Hemet turned into a town with high crime, prostitution and high taxes. Seeking a better life for my son and family, we moved to Utah. To start my new life meant leaving behind my job as a meat wrapper for Vons, everyone and everything familiar to me.

Packing up the Ryder and driving to Utah was exciting at first. We had planned the move for some time, but I don't think I was ready for what came next. Finding myself in a quaint little town, hundreds of miles from friends and family, I felt like a fish out of water. Everything familiar to me was gone and I found myself isolated and lonely. I took my questions to God and asked him many times, 'What's next?'

What value could I bring to the workforce now? After all, I had the same job for 25 years. There were a few things that job taught me that would serve me well as a cook and in the kitchen. I had good knife skills and a vast knowledge of meat and seafood. I was also taught every cut of meat and how to cut it properly. A good place to start.

I thought "that's where I'll start." Taking my positive attitude, big smile and happy-go-lucky spirit, I hit the ground running.

There were many opportunities to cook that just seemed to come my way. Looking back, I believe God was in my corner and opened doors for me right and left. I took every job opportunity and pursued them with a vengeance.

Being a woman in a man's world, especially in a kitchen setting where men usually hold the executive chef positions, I had to close my ears to the ego and negative talk, and learn to push forward in confidence.

I listened intently to the chef in charge and soaked it all in. I had a thirst for knowledge and the desire to learn everything I could. Every spare minute was spent researching. YouTube was a remarkable learning tool, as was reading recipe books and watching cooking shows. As my knowledge of cooking grew, so did my love for the clients and staff I served.

Magic happens when you find your true calling. No matter how long the hours or how difficult the task, they seem easier when you love what you do, and whom you serve.

I had finally found something that lit a fire under me. I had found my true calling as a recovery-center chef. Spending many days, hours and years cooking, I became well-versed in many different recipes and procedures. It's not all about the degree in your hand or the knowledge in your head, it's about a positive attitude and willingness to learn, listen and work hard. All that hard work and long hours paid off: the last five years before retirement, I rose through the ranks and became an executive chef running two different kitchens.

After 46 years in the workforce and turning 62, I decided to hang up my knives and retire from The Chateau Recovery Center.

Retirement should be the best time of your life, but I found myself isolated and lonely, once again. I couldn't depend on my husband's hobbies and interests to keep me happy. I had to find my own way, but what? I found my mind blank of any insight and answers.

The answer came to me in a dream in the early hours of the night, a pivotal moment that rattled me awake. It said, "Jill, you've spent your whole life learning, growing and recreating yourself, don't stop now. Now's the time to do the things you want to do, pursue new avenues and enjoy the ones you love." So, I dove into a couple new projects like writing a chapter in this book, getting my first headshot, taking care of my aging mother and spending more time with my family. The awakening changed my whole outlook on retirement. Now I'm looking forward to what's ahead of me.

You know how you just feel called to do something? I do, and I definitely was.

Before retirement and soon after the covid pandemic hit and the world was in lock down, I was feeling saddened, frustrated and helpless about what was going on in the world. I asked God what I could do? How can I share the message of finding hope in each new day when the world around us is crumbling?

My mind and soul were inspired to share gorgeous photos

of sunrises from around the world. I was being led to remind us all of the beauty in our world – one which appears with the start of every new day. I started a hashtag and called it #sunrisearoundtheworld.

The LinkedIn platform made it accessible to everyone around the world with 689 awesome followers. The #sunrisearountheworld has been going for three inspiring years. To this day, people send photos for me to post. I share with them a positive quote written by a woman with true inspiration, Linda Lane. It's been an inspiring journey.

I have received many letters about how much #sunrisearoundtheworld changed their perspective and made them feel happy again. We may never know the joy we've brought to someone until they tell us.

Hamadi Sowe writes from Gambia:
"It's a pleasure to share with you Jill. I've always been overcome by kindness and love since we met. You've been kind and lovely and I really appreciate that in a person. It's very Paramount to treat each other like humans and then like a family. Some people are very arrogant and don't have respect for others. That's all I hate in life. So, once again I'm deeply pleased to meet you and share like friends and family; thanks for being you. Acts of kindness can make the world a happier place for everyone. Kindness can boost feelings of confidence, being in control, happiness and optimism. Kindness also encourages others to repeat the Good Deeds they've experienced themselves. It contributes to a more positive community."

My hope Is that somehow, I've inspired you to listen to that Inner voice that guides you. Don't be afraid of what's next, have faith in yourself and your abilities. You can do anything you set your mind to.

There will never be that perfect time or perfect circumstance, and you will never have all the answers laid out before you. It is possible to accomplish your goals and dreams if you will just jump in and believe in yourself.

My message has always been that with hard work and perseverance anything is possible.

This is one of my favorite quotes by Helen Keller:

"I am one, but still, I am one. I cannot do everything, but still, I can do something and because I cannot do everything, I will not refuse to do the something that I can do."
Helen Keller

That quote became my work motto, and is the driving force behind #sunrisearoundtheworld.

An illness left Helen Keller unable to see, hear or speak. Keller lived most of her early years without a means of communicating with those around her. With the help of her teacher, Annie Sullivan, Keller underwent a transformation and learning. It was Anne's ability to reach Keller and tap into her great potential that changed her life forever. She went on to advocate for the blind, for women's suffrage, and also co-founded the American civil liberties Union.

"The reward for our work is not what we get, but what we become."

I would like to dedicate my chapter in this book to my grandkids, Bryan and Ruby Shumway, whom I love very much.

Jill Sullivan is on a mission to share hope in each new day and that a new world of possibilities is for the taking with each new glorious sunrise.

No matter the difficulty or struggles we are all going through, it's possible to come out of it and create a new life, a new you.
She is a retired executive chef who enjoys serving others, and sharing her love for nutritious and healthy food.

Connect with her on LinkedIn: Chef(Sully)Jill Sullivan

STILL SO MUCH LIFE TO LIVE
~CHRIS FREER

I guess there was more for me to do than toss myself under the next truck. Somehow, I managed to get myself out of that bad decision. I could make the most of my life despite physical challenges and the system that failed me.

The neurologist delivered the news. "Mr. Freer, you have Multiple Sclerosis." We have disease modifying drugs (DMDs) that slow the progress and you should be able to live a normal life for many years to come. He told me to limit exercise. And that was about the only advice I got. This proved not to be the case for me. My whole life had fallen down around my ears, and I was finding it hard to work. My first marriage was about to end in divorce, and I really felt I had nothing to live for. How wrong I was.

A thought prevented me from going under the front wheels of that truck and saved me that day. As I saw the driver of the truck thundering towards me, I had a sense of compassion for him. I wondered what effect my action would have on his life. That thought stopped me going under the front wheels and caused me to glance off the side of his vehicle, instead.

The events which led me to think it was a good idea to end my life can only be described as chaos and confusion. Anxiety became a regular feature in my daily life. The only way I can describe that anxiety was as if an orchestra had all decided to tune their instruments at the same time. I think there may have been a rock band thrown in there for good measure. However, as I lay there on the grass easement, bruised but alive, I had this moment of clarity, the orchestra sat patiently waiting for the conductor to start; the rock band had moved on to their next gig!

The force of the truck had blown me backwards, onto the grass verge. As I lay there thinking wow that hurt, I could hear a bird singing in the distance. Such a beautiful moment! For the first time in a long while I had a sense of clarity, clear thinking. As I'm sure you can appreciate, I needed some help! Which I received from my local hospital. Fortunately, no broken bones, just bruising. And of course, I had to see the psychiatrist who wanted to section me.

This did not happen, because a family member agreed to take me into their home and keep an eye on me. The confusion and chaos had come to an end and I had a burning question in my mind. Why did I have compassion for the lorry driver and none for myself, my children, and all those people that knew and cared about me?

I was aware I had hit rock bottom. However, solid rock seemed like a good foundation to start to rebuild my life. There was only one way I could go and it was up. Around that time my neurologist, seeing how the illness had progressed, ordered an enhanced MRI scan. The results showed I had many new lesions in my brain and in his opinion, I had reached the secondary progressive stage which happens with this progressive disease.

Unfortunately, there were no DMDs available for secondary progressive Multiple Sclerosis. He also suggested in light of my mental health issues, I should resign myself to the fact that I would be in a wheelchair. Now I know this news may well sound negative but somehow, I felt challenged by that news. Challenged in a good way! I had nothing to lose now and everything to gain. My mindset changed and I started to actively look for positive stories relating to the condition I had. To my surprise I found there were people living proactively with this condition, and I wanted to be like them.

At this point I would like to take you back to the year 1959, the year of my birth. My entrance into the world came 10 years after my brother was born. My mother desperately wanted another child, but sadly she had several miscarriages before my arrival. As you can probably appreciate, she was not in the best state of health when she fell pregnant with me. Doctors at the time advised my mother to terminate the pregnancy simply because, in their opinion, only one of us would survive.

Nevertheless, she stuck to her guns and was determined to continue. I think this was in some way responsible for the poor relationship I had with my father. I am sure he was worried that he would be facing yet another miscarriage and all the sadness that comes attached to an event like that. Or perhaps the worst-case scenario, two children and no wife. Which back then would have been a very hard situation to face.

Anyway, the reality was we both survived. I was premature and spent some time in hospital before I was allowed home, but I was alive. In fact, my mother went on to outlive my dad by many years and reached the age of 86. This is the first point I want to make. In no way do I want to make you think I am an anti-health professional, I am not. However, if my mother had taken their advice, and not been so adamant that she would proceed with the pregnancy, I would not be here!

This highlighted to me that I had resilience, a born survivor. There was also a feeling that they could be wrong. Why was the neurologist right? He could be wrong this time when he said I would be in a wheelchair? It was true I was using the chair for most of my time spent outdoors. but I still had some function. Why not focus on what I could do and improve it. It was possible because he said that would be the outcome my actions were creating that reality.

I had already changed many of my daily choices. There has been a drastic change in my diet. Eliminating foods that were causing inflammation. I was focusing on what I could do and making sure I was moving my limbs as often as I could. Meditation or simply being in the present moment became a daily practice. There was still something missing! I was not sure what it was and then it happened! My rattled awake moment! How did I get MS? You don't catch it; I am not infectious; you cannot catch MS from me. I do understand there are theories attached to MS but no one really knows. With that said, I decided to uncreate that environment that had allowed this illness to take up residency within my body, it became an unwelcome guest.

My belief about our innate power to heal changed, I could heal my body. That shift was the missing piece I needed to complete the puzzle. Slowly I got feeling back into my toes, I started to be able to wiggle them.

These signs spurred me on and empowered me towards my

goal, to walk again! Which I am pleased to be able to tell you I have achieved. For me MS has in the end been a positive force in my life. Yes, I know it is a strange thing to say but it has. I am now in my 64th year of life and I am probably fitter now with it than I was without it. Which in case you are wondering has been over 20 years. To me MS is like that best mate, we all have one. That mate who we don't have to see for years but when we do see them, we just pick it up from where we left off.

I do have a point and I hope it is becoming clear to you. My health outcome has been greatly improved by looking at the choices I made. Most of those choices were unhealthy ones. My belief about health kept me trapped. That belief was that we had very little control and I put my trust in the health profession to fix me when something went wrong. I think I have given you two examples of why this is not always the case. I have already said we should follow their advice but don't blindly rely on that course of action. It does not have to be the only approach. We have a chronic health condition explosion in western society. Chronic health problems are becoming an everyday occurrence for many. Our health systems are keeping people alive but in a state of ill health. Rates of type 2 diabetes are skyrocketing. There are an increasing number of people being overweight. Being overweight is a precursor to poor health. Being overweight is the first step to developing a chronic health condition. Something needs to change. New thinking is needed. That investment in prevention starts with you! We all have the power to choose, please make sure you start making healthy choices.

Before the 1880s it was a widely held belief that illnesses, like Cholera and the plague, were spread by Miasma, or, bad smells. Thankfully, in 1876, Robert Koch proved bacteria were responsible for causing these terrible diseases.

Lifestyle choices is the common denominator involved in most health conditions we see today. This is our "Miasma" moment guys. Wake up and smell the roses!

My rattled awake moment happened when I realized I did not catch MS. I have created a different outcome by getting real and honest about the way I had and was living my life. The choices I made had a profound effect on my wellbeing. I hope the book will encourage others towards their best health. I am living proof lifestyle works, wheelchair to walking.

Now, I am on a mission to empower as many people as possible towards their best health. Join me on this journey and become a happier, healthier human!

Are you ready for your rattled awake moment?

Chris Freer is on a mission to encourage others towards their best health, mental and physical. He does this by first drawing on his own lived experience. He has lived with a diagnosis multiple sclerosis for over 20 years.
He is a qualified hypnotherapist and coach who Is happy speaking at events, public and online. He has taken back his body's ability to heal. Achieving wheelchair to walking living proactively with a chronic health condition. You can find him here:
linkedin.com/in/chris-freer-2109a7149

NOT A "COUGAR" OR A "KAREN" ~ERIKA WARFIELD

Not a "Cougar" or a "Karen" and Worth WAY More than 9 Pence...

CART MASTER: Bring out your dead! *[clang]*
CUSTOMER: Here's one.
CART MASTER: Nine pence.
DEAD PERSON: I'm not dead!
CUSTOMER: Yes, he is.
DEAD PERSON: I'm not!
CART MASTER: He isn't?
CUSTOMER: Well, he will be soon. He's very ill.
DEAD PERSON: I'm getting better!
CUSTOMER: No, you're not. You'll be stone dead in a moment.

And, there it is...

Monty Python summing up what it's like to be a woman once you hit 40.

If you had told me I had a "best-by date" at 44, my 17-year-old self would have humbled you in the only way a secular GenX teenager would: "Get bent."

(I cleaned that up for you.)

Yet, society has their opinions (all of them equally as crass as "get bent") when it comes to women between the ages of 40 and 80. Forget any grace when it comes to an older woman with a husband 22 years younger. Oh, Lawdy! You have to be an emotionally nimble person to put up with other people's small-mindedness.

Too bad for society that it's still getting it wrong on GenX gals.

Play stupid games. Win stupid prizes.

Supermodel Paulina Porizkova sums it up **_best_**: We get shoved into a big black hole.

Personally, I think we get shoved in harder if we choose to age gracefully without cosmetic surgeries, hair dye, and fillers.

Yet, like the "Holy Grail" peasant, we're not dead yet. Not even close.

And, we're certainly worth more than 9 pence. In fact, we're worth more than rubies and fine gold.

But most of society would have us believe we need to:

- Sit down.
- Shut up.
- Our wisdom matters not.
- We're past our "expiration date".
- Nobody cares.
- Give it up, Granny.

That's a whole lot of other people's trauma and toxicity coming our way.

As we say in the South:
> "Not my pasture. Not my bull$#*t."

And, those of you gorgeous Millennials "aging out", take heed. This "Logan's Run" nonsense awaits you, too…
IF we don't start supporting each other as women in radical self-acceptance regarding the beauty of aging.

So, what was it that woke me up besides turning 44?

Long story short:

A brutal marriage, followed by a blissful divorce from an "age-appropriate" man, who openly admitted in counseling that the only reason he married me was this…

"She was pretty, and I thought she'd be good for business."

Narcissism at its finest.

It was a glorious moment, though, for reasons he couldn't fathom.

The second he stopped reveling in the sound of his own voice, I heard God say in His own perfect, loving whisper:

"Do not mourn what never existed."

I was free. The man for whom I had waited until our wedding day just admitted that none of our married life and covenant was real. It didn't exist. All of it was lies.
I was free to show myself mercy and grace for believing his every deceit.

From that day, I never mourned. Instead, I rejoiced over my body healing from several illnesses brought on by the stress of that marriage.

One illness was so severe, a male OB/GYN wanted to remove my uterus and ovaries because there was "no point to them at my age".

Right. No point except they're a part of my endocrine system. And, taking them out didn't solve the root cause. At this time, I was a Christ-follower, so I *politely* told him to get bent.

Seeing a theme in how women past 40 get treated?

We're "old bags" who deserve to have our internal "bags" removed to increase our future health problems and doctors' revenues.

However, as I healed without my male OB/GYN's assistance, God's lesson would serve me in unbelievable ways.

Everyday, I began living for myself and for God.

I could never have done that if I was stuck lamenting over things that never existed.

How many of us stop living because we're mourning what never existed?

Replaying the lies we believed on a vicious loop.
Replaying narratives society wrote for us as women (like just get rid of your uterus because there's "no point" in keeping it).

With every new betrayal over the next 8 years, I heard God's words again.

"Do not mourn what never existed."

It became my mantra. It saved my mental health time and again.

The far end of the Narcissistic Spectrum is becoming quite congested with people invested in us buying their narratives or succumbing to their smear campaigns when we don't.

Never forget: You are glorious. You are valid. You are beautiful. You are wise… and your wisdom is hard-freakin'-earned.

But nothing tested my mantra more than how society treats older women in relationships with younger men… or more specifically men who aren't "age-appropriate".

Society is totally FINE with older men / younger women…

Well, unless you're a slovenly Leonardo DiCaprio dating a drop-dead gorgeous 19-year-old sugar baby.

I think people are starting to wake up a bit on that count.

For me, after my divorce I was fully prepared to become the world's first Protestant Nun. Guns blazing. I was on fire not to get married ever again.

Then God decided to unleash his sense of humor in the middle of my ballroom dance class.

The man who was to become my future husband walked in. He was 22 thinking I was 27. I was 44 hoping he was at least 27.

All doubt as to his age was erased when he proceeded to tell this intermediate-level dancer that I was dancing the Rumba incorrectly, when it was his first time in a dance class.

My answers to his forthcoming pursuit were immediate:

- "NO, I could have birthed you."
- "I'm not one of those cougars."

- "Go away, kid. You're bothering me."
- And, what I thought would be the nail in his coffin – "I believe in abstinence and waiting for marriage."

Well. It wasn't the nail in his coffin. He actually agreed with that last one. Even after many conversations confirming that all the workarounds the younger generations use are still... in fact... sex before marriage.

We eventually did begin dating with some very clear boundaries set. Many too numerous to detail in just this chapter.
All of them set with the full knowledge that society would judge me more harshly than him.

Facts.

And believe me when I say society did judge me more harshly... regardless of how we both believed in and were committed to abstinence.

Our friendship needed to pass the test without all the other garbage that society would foist upon us about the "cougar" nonsense.

That and sometimes, we as women simply need to realize our partners need that time to heal too, as we heal ourselves.

We heard it all:

- A 65-year-old, wealthy, Low-Testosterone, AARP-eligible, confirmed bachelor telling me I needed to date "age appropriate" men, as he himself had recently dated a woman younger than me.
- My boyfriend being teased for "dating his mom" or for being a "big-game hunter" and then being asked

> what I was like in bed, or worse theories offered to him.

- Being accused publicly at a party in front of business people that we were sleeping together, because being abstinent was not possible.
- And, then the pièce de résistance from a self-professed Christian woman… if you're not sleeping together, "there must be something wrong with her vagina."

You may resume blinking now.

Ladies, you heard it here first in dating a younger man… you will be darned if you do and darned if you don't.
If anything, all the hate made us stronger as a couple and as friends. So much so that we did marry almost 4 years later. And, we did wait for our wedding day.

I asked my now-husband when we were dating why he was staying in the onslaught of vicious projection, gaslighting, objectification, and judgment.

His answer?

"Because the girls I've dealt with at my age want to be saved. They say they aren't victims, then proceed to act like victims. They don't have their stuff together even though they think they do. They're all over the place. They've all used sex as a weapon."

Think about that.

Ironically, I'm not necessarily an advocate for dating younger men. My story ain't about "How Stella Got Her Groove Back". Far from it. That older woman / younger man trope is tired and played out.

What I am an advocate for is being open-minded and having the discernment to know when you are in the presence of one who is mature beyond their years and just GETS IT.

Gets that being with an older woman is like having your own sage with a wisdom that is beneficial and to be revered.

Gets that our sparkles (gray hairs) are a sign of beauty and profound knowledge.

Gets that wrinkles show a life well-lived if we allow that to be.

If you're a survivor of divorce or of society's toxic black hole, know that whatever the small-minded throw your way is not only survivable, their facade of "reason" DOES NOT EXIST.

What existed for me was God's wisdom.

And, it took God's wisdom through my much younger husband to show me the power of true friendship in marriage.

It's time for us to blow up society's scriptwriting. These jokers are worse at scriptwriting than Hollywood (if that's even possible).

It's time to understand God's script and the greatness He placed in us, because:

- You are valid, you are seen, you are heard, you are wise, powerful, and beautiful.
- You deserve the grace and the gift of healing. You deserve your own script without society's interference.

- You are a force to be reckoned with, possessing a discernment and wisdom that should be revered in the way that our ancestors did in previous generations.

It may just be that we GenX gals are the ones to reclaim all of that and pass it down to future generations of women.

Let those who continue to judge us keep their stupid prizes.

Erika Warfield is on a mission to help GenX women avoid society's toxic black hole. That black hole is the effort to silence, project, gaslight, objectify, and sideline older women as they enter their peak in power, beauty, wisdom, and grace. She does so with humor and a "No-BS" style of servant leadership. Erika and her (much younger) husband assist others in achieving their own levels of peak performance. You can find her on online at: https://www.linkedin.com/in/erikawarfield/.

REMARKABLE COMEBACKS
~LEEANNA STOCK-LUOMA

Transfer your Setbacks into Remarkable Comebacks

It's easy to dismiss the notion as trite – the idea that you can make magic out of your mess. Yet, against all odds, this familiar phrase holds a deep truth. I cannot wait to tell you about the story of my website, its God-send of an origin story, and how I can help people just like you travel the path that I am on, and have been on, for a very long time.

It stinks to feel like crap. It really does.

We all know what it's like to struggle and feel like everything is falling apart. Those moments when we're at our lowest, yet we put on a brave face and pretend everything is fine, even when it's far from it.

"How are you?" A simple question we encounter daily. And what's our usual response? "I'm fine."

But are we really always fine? The truth is, we're not. When someone asks me how I'm doing, I simply reply, "I'm still kicking." The irony will make you laugh…

The story I'm about to share begins with a diagnosis of multiple sclerosis (MS) just as I was graduating from high school. A vibrant and active student, I captained the track team, excelled in volleyball, starred in school productions, participated in both Honor and Homecoming Court, and was deeply involved in the community. My world was rocked by the news of a disease I had never considered.

When I was first diagnosed, I would get steroid injections, which would bring me back to "normal" and I could function at 100%. I had my mind set on attending college, and, despite my diagnosis, I set forth on my new adventure.

I earned a bachelor's degree in Health Education from the University of Minnesota, Duluth, and after obtaining my degree, enrolled in a graduate program at a second college. The University of Wisconsin, Superior, is a widespread campus. Graduate school beckoned, yet the harsh winters of a widespread campus posed a significant hurdle. I would have had to park quite a distance from my classes, and walk through the snow and cold. Anyone who has ever been to Duluth and the Twin Ports area knows that the winters can be downright nasty! After considering my options, I decided to attend a nearby school that had a smaller campus.

It was at the College of Saint Scholastica where I met two inspiring professors that were dietitians. Their impact led me to a new path, and I spent three more years pursuing a second bachelor's degree in Dietetics, Food, and Nutrition. Upon completion of this program, I was required to complete an internship, and I was thrilled when I was accepted to the prestigious Mayo Clinic in Rochester, Minnesota. This led to expanding my education at the Mayo School of Health Related Sciences for another year, where I learned and grew in my career.

Reflecting back on my time as a dietitian and diabetes educator, there are many relationships with my clients that I cherished. I once had a client, who we will call Penny, who was very depressed. She had been overweight her whole life, and she came to me for education and counseling to receive bariatric surgery for weight loss. I worked with her for over six months, and I watched someone emerge from the darkness. She was happy. She no longer blamed herself. Witnessing transformations like Penny's – a journey from darkness to light, just goes to show that things do get better, despite the challenges faced. At the end of Penny's journey, she hugged me and thanked me over and over. She had a picture of us together and made a poster board of sorts, and titled it, "My journey." She proudly asked me to display her success in my office. While she gave me all the credit, I reminded her that she did all of the work. She transformed her lifelong setback into a remarkable comeback.

Life's journey is paved with roadblocks, and each time, I found my way back stronger. The disease progression caused my feet to contract, which led to excruciating pain in my feet, robbing me, and my husband, of sleep. In August of 2019, a bilateral ankle and foot surgery was completed to alleviate the pain and correct the problem. Following the procedure, my plan was to return to work with casts on my legs, and to continue my career as a dietitian and diabetes care specialist.

As we know, our plan is not God's plan. Sometimes life's events seem senseless, leaving us questioning, "Why me?" My recovery from surgery faced unexpected challenges, leading to a halt in my nearly 30-year career due to complications. I was forced to quit my job, and soon, the feelings of depression, worthlessness, and defeat became all too familiar. As I grappled with isolation, losing my mom and dog within months of each other, as well as my job, I understood the depths of despair. But amid the rubble of shattered plans, an unexpected opportunity arose.

Out of nowhere, my husband received an email. He had been looking for an available domain, to start a DIY website. Someone from a Facebook website group came out of the blue, and offered him a totally unrelated website. The domain was "dealingwithdiabetes.org." What are the chances? He was looking for nothing of the sort. It was as though God was sending him this email and telling him that this is what I should do! This serendipitous event marked the birth of my chance to educate and support from the comfort of home. The opportunity to start my own website and educate people from home was my "Rattled Awake" moment. I've come back again! I CAN continue to educate and support people, I CAN continue to help people, and I DO make a difference.

Life's journey is a rollercoaster, with peaks and valleys that test us. When setbacks come your way – those unexpected hurdles, difficulties, or bumps in the road that seem to derail your progress – remember that they don't have to define your story. In fact, setbacks can become the very catalyst that propels you towards your remarkable comeback! Imagine setbacks as roadblocks on your path. At first glance, they might seem insurmountable, causing frustration and disappointment.

Consider this: setbacks can be transformed into stepping stones.

I have MS, but I'm not letting MS have me!

Nowadays, when I'm asked how I'm doing, I reply, "I'm still kicking, just not as high as I used to!"

LeeAnna Stock-Luoma is on a mission to continue to educate people with diabetes, despite being diagnosed with multiple sclerosis a young age, and has persevered through life-long roadblocks. Unfortunately, due to multiple complications resulting from foot surgery in 2019, she was forced to leave her career of nearly 30 years. With help and support from friends and family, as well as her faith in God, she has found the inspiration to face the challenges of her disability and pivot her career by launching a new diabetes and nutrition blog. Follow her on LinkedIn: LeeAnna Stock-Luoma RD, LD, CD, CDCES

LOOK BEYOND THE BOX ~SUSANNAH DAWN

"I'm not what I used to be, yet I am who I've always been." Susannah Dawn

Look Beyond the Box, For We Are So Much More

We live life to the fullest when we do so as the person we were created to be, who we are in our soul. However, once we are placed in boxes, it all begins to unravel.

Each box – each label – is used to define who we are by those who put us there: the Placer. We become labeled because of some aspect of who we are: neurodiverse; overcame an addiction; have a non-regional accent; fall within the LGBTQ+ community; are of a certain faith; and so many other boxes. Once we are defined in a specific way, the Placer cherry-picks an example from a subset of those in the group that fits their desired narrative, and then paints everyone in that box with that same paintbrush.

There are two flaws to that reasoning. First, everyone labeled as "____" is a unique individual, and everyone in that box is as diverse as the rest of the country. Sharing a similar attribute in no way means everyone is the same, nor that they are aligned with everyone else in that group – or even views themselves belonging there.
Second, no label can accurately or fully describe an

individual; each of us is so much more than any box in which a Placer might put us could ever describe.

I understand this well, having been stuck in boxes all my life. It led me to withdraw from everyone and become an entrenched introvert most of my life. From early childhood, my dad told me who and what I was based on a simple attribute. I knew who I was better than he did. However, when relaying my goals and dreams, Dad and other Placers told me what I should be and do based solely on how they viewed me; how failing to follow their guidance would lead to bad things happening in my life.

The thing is, by the age of three, I knew the truth of who I am... I went to bed every night praying to God that I would wake up a girl. I understood who I was in my soul, even though my body told people I was a boy. It was when my dad caught me playing dress-up that he spanked me and began to make comments alluding to how anything girlish was bad. It was his attempt to squash any semblance of girlishness from me... to cure me.

He failed. His efforts only led to further fear of, and pulling away from, him. Being so young, I couldn't articulate why I knew I was a girl. Thus, once I hit the wall of rejection to who I really was, it was no longer possible to open up and tell anyone how I felt.

It would be a half-century before I was able to step forth into the world as my authentic self. My reinvention to live life aligned with my soul began in a Sephora store the day after Christmas, 2019.

It was there that God began to open doors by placing women in my path who saw – and accepted – me for who I was at my core. It was there I felt encouraged to open up in ways I'd never felt safe doing during the previous half-century of my life. While always glad to answer my skincare and makeup questions, my connection with each lady grew as we began to talk about ourselves in the manner of close friends. It was a new experience for me. Everyone who was close to me and knew about my reinvention commented how they not only saw the physical changes, they saw how I looked more and more confident and poised each time they saw me. I understood how the Lord put women in my life whom I needed, ladies I could trust and would help to strengthen His armor around me in preparation for the times I would need it.

One of the first tests of my strengthened armor was the day I stood before my dad and told him the truth… to state who I was and how I had always known.

Before you begin to think this is just another trans story, understand that so many of us go through similar situations in our lives, all because of who we are: the woman who has a non-regional accent and tries to hide it for fear that she would be stereotyped because of where she's from; the man who overcame alcohol addiction and worries what would happen if his co-workers found out. We all have aspects of ourselves we hide for fear of what others might say or do… how they may treat us differently. Yet, when we hide, we are also less likely to meaningfully engage with others.

The last day of June 2021, was one of the harshest of my life. It was the day I opened up and told my dad who I was at my core, revealing my authentic self.
"You didn't have to tell me," he said. "You know where you're headed." Those were his first words. It didn't matter

to him that faith was my foundation, or that I saw prayers answered as doors I thought were locked began to open. Instead, Dad placed me in a box that fit the narrative he chose to believe.

The conversation following those words was purely one-sided. Yes, I responded to his questions and comments, yet he refused to accept anything I said. Every word he spoke was progressively harsh, dripping with an agonizing venom that penetrated deep into my core.

Then he said something for which my reply had been prepared in my heart long ago.

I knew my dad had a response at the ready when he made the statement... envisioned it as if he held a double-barreled shotgun in his lap, with both barrels loaded, cocked... his finger on the trigger, ready to blast me with his reply.

"So, I guess God made a mistake."

Those were his words. Simply spoken, yet potentially explosive.

I calmly looked him in the eyes, "God doesn't make mistakes."

The conversation was over.

For one of the first times in my life, over a half-century of being his child, I stood my ground. I didn't back down in his presence as I usually did, as I had done since age seven.

I was placed in a box with negative connotations by my dad. How he viewed me... the words he spoke... the entire experience was trying to pull me under the waves, back into the dark depths of the murky sea that was my past. The chains were thick and heavy, fueling the pain and anguish I felt over the next few days as they tugged at me. Tears of pain from how he hurt me with his words flowed without any warning, thereby keeping me home for days.

At the same time, I remembered something that was able to cut the chains of the past: forgiveness.

This concept is often misunderstood. Too often we either waste time waiting for an apology, or believe we need to tell the person who harmed us that they are forgiven. The truth of forgiveness is how it is for us... to forgive from the heart allows us to cut those chains and begin to heal. No conversation is necessary, especially as those we forgive are likely to believe they did nothing wrong.

Once I opened my heart to forgive my dad, the healing process began. I accepted who he was, his upbringing, and that it was likely he would never accept me. My focus on this created a process by which I was able to heal over a few days. Without forgiveness, I may still be experiencing the full pain from that conversation.

Again, many people experience similar situations in their lives: the teenage girl who was pregnant and turned out of her parents' home; the son who comes out to his father as gay and is immediately rejected; the child who converts to another faith and is shunned by family and friends. Though the situations may differ, many people have similar encounters in their lives.

As much as that conversation with Dad shook me, it also prepared me for the biggest challenge I would face only six weeks later... from someone close to me who claimed to be my biggest supporter.

This person, I will call them Robin, was in town for a few weeks on a project. They asked if they could stay in my house a few nights, and I was happy to say yes. It was when they asked if I'd let a man stay with them at my house, was when the situation started to go bad.

"I don't know this person, and – in all honesty – strange men make me very uncomfortable... I don't feel safe right now if, for any reason, I find myself alone in the house with strangers."

When I mentioned to my manicurist what had happened a few days later, she said, "I know it shouldn't be that way, but most of us women have a fear of men."

Robin refused to accept that no meant no, and pushed back. Stopping by the house with flowers, as she knew it was the first anniversary of my mom's passing from Alzheimer's, they told me how he was a nice guy, bi, and had come out to his parents. My first thought was, *"So what?"* All I felt was how they ignored my feelings, seeming to not care about my fear of men and how the situation didn't feel right to me.

I felt claustrophobic in the box in which Robin viewed me. My dad put me in a box where he painted everyone as fitting the same negative narrative. Robin put me in a similar box, with a narrative point of view of everyone being the same... and that they should all have the same interests and want to meet and hang out with everyone in that box.

Both viewed me as just another LGBTQ+ / trans person... as if that's how I identified myself.

I never "identified" as trans or female. I've known since the age of three that I am... that my soul is... female. I've only ever seen myself as a woman. Instead, because of my dad, I spent half-century feeling like an imposter trying to identify as male because of my non-aligned shell.

And so, a couple days later, Robin made another attempt to get me to let their friend stay in my home. I received a text telling me, "He's also dated trans people and is a very good listener & support & resource!" Obviously *"no"* to Robin meant *"keep trying until she says yes."* Instead of easing my concerns, however, what I saw in the message was that Robin violated a basic trust.

I was devastated.

I realized Robin outed me to the man, a total stranger! The most basic trust I had in someone who always said they were supportive of me evaporated in a split second. The pain running through me at that moment was more agonizing than anything I'd ever experienced, including my dad's words earlier that summer. I felt violated in so many ways that it was difficult to comprehend them all, flowing over and through me like a waterfall dropping me into major rolling rapids. In a single moment, I felt more alone in the universe than at any time hidden away in my closet those five decades.

I dropped to the floor in tears. My concerns, my fears, meant nothing to Robin. They outed me, and I felt violated in a way I'd never felt in my life.
Someone I trusted had not only outed me, their actions made me feel unsafe in my own house, and for what? Just so they could have some man – whom I feared – be allowed to stay with them in my house? How did that make any sense?

After letting Robin know their comments actually increased my sense of being threatened, I wrote, "However, what I'm most concerned about is that you told him about me, you outed me, and I've been in tears from the moment I realized that." I made it clear I needed to be alone with no guests in the house.

That first night was rough. Unsure if Robin would respect my wishes, I locked my bedroom door as a safety precaution. I cried myself to sleep, curled up tightly in a fetal position as a deep sense of abuse permeated through my body. When I awoke in the morning, I felt a little better, at least until seeing Robin's response. "Sorry to hear this," was followed by their claim of trying to help me, noting how they knew I was going through a hard time due to the anniversary of my mom's passing. There was no denial of outing me.

While the pain refused to go away, I knew what I had to do to heal. In my heart I forgave Robin… accepted them for who they were at that moment, knowing how important a step it was for me to take so I could move forward with my own personal healing. Still, over the next few weeks, and at unexpected moments, I would cry uncontrollably, curled up into a ball to protect myself – even alone in my own home.

Never let it be said that words don't hurt, as I was hurt deeply by words that summer. Yet, through forgiveness – and acceptance – of both my dad and Robin, I healed.
Yes, it took much longer to heal after Robin than it did after talking with my dad. However, as with healing from the wounds caused by my dad's harsh words, I emerged stronger from the pain received through Robin's words

using the same process.

It was after these encounters that two important lessons were placed on my heart. The first was an understanding of the reason I was allowed to be hurt so deeply. For most of my life, it was crucial for me to hide my authentic self. By staying behind the walls I had meticulously built brick-by-brick around me… another box, if you will… they insulated me from painful experiences that many people experienced in their lives for a myriad of reasons. By going through both of those events… the verbal rejection of a parent, and the breach of trust from my biggest supporter, I have an experienced understanding of the pains others suffered at similar times in their lives.

During the days following my dad's verbal assault, when he completely rejected everything about who I am, I felt what it was like to feel so worthless that it would have been easy to believe ending this existence was best for everyone.

It was similar to how I felt during my previous marriage, when the verbal assault on me by my ex had me wishing to be removed from life so as to no longer be a bother to others. Even so, feeling such vitriol from a parent was almost too much to bear, even at my age. I understood at a deep level why so many children and young adults who felt similar sentiments from their parents, for any number of reasons, chose to attempt to depart this existence – with too many succeeding.

The second was focused on the boxes others put us in to label us, and thereby control us. All too often we are sequestered in them because of how others view the group as a whole, based on a believed narrative, instead of seeing the individuals as unique Humans. Truth is, the boxes don't exist. When we are in them, it is a fear that holds us back, seducing us to believe we would not be safe should we move beyond them… a fear that knows all of our lived experiences and how to weave such grains of truth within its translucent web of lies.

Both my dad and Robin placed me in a box, and the fear within tried to keep me in its grasp. Yes, both of them viewed me as belonging to a group of individuals with whom each believed were all alike. Yet, to be identified as trans had so many negative connotations, similar to how someone who was neurodiverse, LGBTQ+, had mental health diagnoses, or numerous other "labeled" people might feel. I heard how my fear said to accept how others viewed me and, since it knew I didn't like that feeling, remained hidden within the safety of its walls.

However, we are all so much more than the box others – or we – place us in. To move beyond the box is to own the box, to own our fear… for, when we own our fear, fear no longer owns us. Then, as our awareness is ignited, we can see our path and take the first step. No matter how big or small it is, it becomes the first step towards our freedom… the first step in moving beyond the box.

We must also recognize that we are never truly isolated. While it was all too easy to slip into solitude after each encounter, the past few years brought remarkable women into my life. They revealed a deep power of trust with me… through which came confirmation of how they had my back. Those incredible women of Sephora enlightened me how, despite the shadows cast by fear and negativity, there were still moments… beautiful, radiant moments… where I basked in total acceptance. It was during those priceless moments when the boxes… the barriers trying to hold me back… dissolved, leaving only the bonds of shared experience… and the artistry of their brushes.

Susannah Dawn is on a mission to lift women beyond the boxes they feel stuck in to shine as their authentic selves. She speaks at length on the importance of women being their authentic selves. She has both an upcoming memoir and fantasy duology that speak at length on this topic. You can find her here:

https://linktr.ee/susannah.dawn.

BENEATH THE PERFECT SCORE ~DR. CONSTANCE LEYLAND

Beneath the Perfect Score: The Silent Crisis of Student Suicides in Asian Cultures

In the pursuit of academic excellence, the world has often looked to Asian cultures as paragons of dedication and discipline. However, beneath the surface of this reverence lies a growing concern: an alarming increase in suicide rates among Asian students. This tragic trend raises profound questions about the immense cultural pressures placed upon young shoulders striving to meet the demanding standards of being an 'A' student.

An Early Stage

In the early chapters of my life, abandonment became the haunting melody that echoed through the corridors of my existence. At the tender age of two, I was cast adrift into a world of uncertainty, as my parents made the heart-wrenching decision to leave me behind. Their departure, the first and most vivid memory of my childhood, marked the inception of a lifelong journey filled with unexpected twists and heartrending crescendos.

Growing up, I found myself dancing to a unique tune, one that was shaped by the cultural backdrop of my Asian

heritage. In this symphony of existence, the pursuit of academic excellence was not merely an aspiration; it was an unwavering expectation, a relentless demand. From the moment I entered the hallowed halls of education, I bore the weight of familial dreams and aspirations,
for being 'number one' was not just an ambition; it was the bridge that connected me to the parents I yearned to see once more.

As I gazed upon their faded photographs, my youthful heart harbored a simple, profound desire—to excel, to achieve that elusive 'number one' spot, in the hope that it would be the beacon guiding me back to their embrace. Each test score, each report card, each accolade—each one held the potential to be my ticket to reunification. The longing to bridge the chasm that had separated us fueled my determination to conquer the academic world.

But little did I know that this pursuit, while noble in its intent, would orchestrate a symphony of its own—a symphony of pressure, sacrifice, and unspoken pain. It was a composition where the relentless pursuit of excellence often overshadowed the tender notes of self-discovery and personal growth.

The echoes of abandonment and the crescendos of academic ambition formed the backdrop of my early years, laying the foundation for the narrative that would unfold. This is the story of how I navigated the intricate score of life, moving from the haunting shadows of abandonment to the profound desire to be 'number one,' and ultimately, to the realization that the most poignant melodies are found in the quiet moments of self-discovery. It is a tale of resilience, transformation, and the quest to understand the complex symphony of one's own existence.

In the annals of education, certain cultures have consistently stood out as exemplars of academic dedication and discipline. Asian societies, in particular, have been lauded worldwide for their reverence toward academic achievement. This admiration, often tinged with envy, stems from the belief that Asian students embody a unique commitment to education, one that seems unparalleled in its intensity.

Setting the Stage: The Reverence for Asian Academic Achievement

To understand the complexities of the rising suicide rates among Asian students, it's imperative to delve into the cultural context that has elevated Asian academic success to legendary status. Asian cultures place a profound emphasis on education, seeing it as not just a path to personal growth but as a means of securing a prosperous future, upholding family honor, and, in some cases, national pride.

Within these societies, the journey to academic excellence is characterized by a relentless pursuit of perfection. The notion of the 'model minority' often places Asian students on a pedestal, perceived as the epitome of diligence, discipline, and academic prowess. But what lies beneath this veneer of success?

The Paradox: Increasing Suicide Rates Among Asian Students

The paradox that haunts these societies is the staggering increase in suicide rates among their own young learners.

On the one hand, we see a culture that venerates education above all else, and on the other, I'm rattled awake by the heartbreaking trend of students succumbing to the immense pressure they face.

This paradox is not merely statistical; it's a heart-wrenching human tragedy. Behind the façade of perfect report cards and exemplary achievements lies a stark reality—the toll this relentless pursuit of excellence takes on the mental and emotional well-being of young students.

Purpose of my Message: To Explore the Root Causes, Consequences, and Solutions

The purpose of my message is to journey through the heart of this paradox. We will peel back the layers to understand the root causes of this silent crisis, examine its consequences on individuals, families, and societies, and seek to unravel the complex web of factors contributing to this alarming trend.

Through research, personal accounts, and a compassionate exploration of the human stories behind the statistics, we aim to shed light on a topic that demands our collective attention. This book is not just an exposé; it's a call to action.

The Asian Educational Myth

We embark on a deep dive into the foundations of the Asian educational myth. We explore the cultural values, traditions, and historical influences that have shaped Asian societies' reverence for academic achievement. We will unpack the pressures and expectations placed on Asian students, both by their families and societies, to excel academically. We will begin to understand why this pursuit of excellence, while noble in its intent, has created an environment ripe for the silent crisis that is plaguing Asian students.

Join us on this journey as we strive to illuminate the shadows of this paradox, one chapter at a time, in our pursuit of a more balanced and compassionate educational landscape.

The Alarming Trends: Expectations and standards for academic performance

As we delve deeper into the labyrinthine world of academic pressures within Asian societies, it becomes evident that the pursuit of educational excellence carries with it a heavy burden—an often invisible weight that has dire consequences for many young souls.

Setting the Cultural Backdrop: The Value of Education in Asian Societies

To truly comprehend the alarming trends we are about to explore, we must first understand the cultural bedrock upon which these pressures are built. **I'm rattled awake** by the realization that education is not merely a stepping stone to success in Asian societies; it is the very foundation upon which life paths are paved.

In Asia, education is revered with a fervor that borders on reverence. It's a shared cultural value, a societal investment, and a source of collective pride. The belief that knowledge is the key to prosperity, personal and familial honor, and national progress is deeply ingrained in the psyche of Asian communities.

From a young age, children are taught to value education as the most potent currency in life's marketplace. It is an investment parents are willing to make at great personal sacrifice, from hiring tutors to funding extracurricular activities and test preparation courses. The value of education transcends generations, carrying the hopes and dreams of parents who yearn for a brighter future for their offspring.

The Pressure Cooker: Expectations and Standards for Academic Performance

Yet, the admiration for education often morphs into a pressure cooker, where the temperature rises relentlessly. The standards for academic performance are set impossibly high, and expectations weigh heavily upon young shoulders.

Consider the burden of acing examinations that determine not just educational paths but also social status and self-worth. In South Korea, the College Scholastic Ability Test (CSAT) is often referred to as "The Gate of Dreams" or "The Final Boss Battle of Adolescence." In Japan, the university entrance exams are akin to a life-or-death battle.

The pursuit of perfection leaves no room for mediocrity. It's a race to the top, where every fraction of a point matters. It's a system where students, some as young as elementary school, juggle hours of homework, after-school classes, and test preparation, often leaving little time for rest, hobbies, or personal growth.

Families invest not only their resources but their emotional well-being into the success of their children.

Parents carry the weight of their children's academic performance as a reflection of their own worth and commitment as caregivers. The pressure to meet familial expectations can be all-consuming.

Examining the 'Model Minority' Stereotype

At the heart of this academic crucible lies a stereotype that, while seemingly flattering, is equally perilous—the 'model minority.' Asian students are often viewed as exemplars of discipline, diligence, and academic prowess. While this stereotype may appear positive, it carries a heavy burden.

The 'model minority' myth sets impossibly high standards for Asian students, expecting them to not just excel academically but also to be perfectly behaved, emotionally resilient, and socially adept. This stereotype can mask the very real struggles and pressures faced by Asian students.

As we journey further into my journey, I'm **rattled awake** by the need to bear in mind the cultural values that place education on a pedestal, the relentless standards for academic performance, and the weight of the 'model minority' stereotype. It is within this complex context that we will unearth the disquieting trends of increasing suicide rates among Asian students—a crisis that calls for our collective attention and compassion.

The Psychological Toll: Statistics and data: A deep dive into rising suicide rates

We delve into the profound psychological toll that the intense academic pressures and rising suicide rates have on Asian students. It's a journey that began with a personal awakening—an awakening that rattled me to my core, making me acutely aware of the urgency of addressing this silent crisis. We'll explore the data, regional variations, and demographic profiles to gain a deeper understanding of the human faces behind these startling statistics.

Statistics and Data: A Deep Dive into Rising Suicide Rates

The statistics surrounding suicide rates among Asian students are undeniably alarming. While it's essential to remember that these numbers represent real lives and stories, they are vital for comprehending the scale of the issue.

In countries like South Korea, Japan, and Singapore, suicide rates among young people have consistently ranked among the highest in the world. These rates are often correlated with the intensity of academic competition and the pressures to succeed in these regions.

In South Korea, for instance, the pressure to excel on the College Scholastic Ability Test (CSAT) has contributed to a suicide rate that has garnered international attention. High-stakes exams and a culture that places a significant emphasis on academic achievement have created a pressure-cooker environment.

Statistical Data:
According to Iwamoto (2019), "Data released in the city-state in July suggests the pressure is indeed mounting. A total of 397 people took their own lives in 2018, up 10% on the year, according to suicide prevention agency Samaritans of Singapore. Boys between the ages of 10 and 19 were particularly at risk, with 19 cases reported -- up from seven in 2017 and the highest number since

1991. "The prevalence of suicide mortality among youths and males is a significant societal concern," the agency said" (para #4).
Reference: Iwamoto, K. (2019). From Singapore to Japan, falling birthrates means fewer siblings and more stress. https://asia.nikkei.com/Spotlight/Asia-Insight/Youth-suicide-Asian-teens-crack-under-growing-family-pressure

According to Organisation for Economic Cooperation and Development (OECD), Korea has the highest suicide rate and reasons given are personal, work, and academic concerns. They are the 12th highest rate of suicide in the world and the highest suicide rate amongst the OECD countries.
Reference: World Health Organization. (n.d.). Suicide rates estimates. For example, South Korea and Japan have faced intense scrutiny due to their exceptionally high suicide rates among students. Singapore, on the other hand, while also dealing with academic pressures, has shown significant efforts in addressing mental health concerns among students. https://apps.who.int/gho/data/node.main.MHSUICIDEASDR?lang=en

These statistics are just a sliver of what lies beneath the surface. Let's look at various Asian countries with the same pressure.

Regional Variations: Contrasting Experiences Across Asian Countries

It's important to note that while the issue of academic pressure and student suicides is widespread in Asia, there are notable variations across countries. Each Asian nation has its unique educational system, cultural values, and societal pressures that contribute to the phenomenon.

Understanding the demographic profile of those most affected by the psychological toll of academic pressures is crucial for tailoring interventions and support systems.

This issue casts its shadow across age groups, but I'm **rattled awake** by the fact that it often emerges most prominently during the formative years of adolescents and young adults. The pursuit of academic excellence aligns with a period of intense personal development and identity formation, rendering these young individuals particularly susceptible to the psychological toll.

Within this demographic, gender disparities surface. In certain Asian societies, a higher incidence of suicide is observed among male students, while in others, females bear a more significant burden. These gender differences can be attributed to prevailing cultural norms, societal expectations, and distinct coping mechanisms.

Additionally, students hailing from disadvantaged socioeconomic backgrounds face added stressors. The weight of economic hardships coupled with limited resources for academic support further compounds the mental health challenges they encounter.

In essence, comprehending the diverse demographic dimensions of this issue is pivotal in crafting targeted strategies that provide the requisite assistance and guidance for those in need.

The Cultural Factors: Mental health and academic pressure: Understanding the link

Let's dive into the cultural aspects that have had a profound impact on the mental health of Asian students, particularly in the context of the relentless academic pressure we've explored.

Mental Health and Academic Pressure: Understanding the Link-The Connection Between Mental Health and Academic Excellence

The link between mental health and the relentless pursuit of academic excellence is intensely personal and something I've witnessed firsthand among my peers. The pressure to excel academically brings a profound psychological burden that often manifests as stress, anxiety, and depression.

Stress: This uninvited companion lingers, a constant presence fueled by the fear of failure, relentless competition, and unceasing expectations. It's akin to a never-ending storm cloud, casting shadows even on our brightest moments.

Anxiety: Anxiety, another unwelcome guest, tightly clenched like a knot in your stomach, paralyzing as exams approach. It makes focusing and performing at your best an almost insurmountable task.

Depression: Often concealed behind a mask of success, depression emerges. The pressure to maintain an image of perfection can lead to a profound sense of hopelessness and isolation. It's like being trapped in a dark room with no discernible way out.

These emotional struggles aren't confined to our minds; they cast a shadow over our physical and cognitive well-being. Stress can lead to headaches, insomnia, and difficulty concentrating. Anxiety can make simple tasks seem insurmountable. Depression drains energy, motivation, and joy in life.

I've personally experienced the palpable toll of stress, the paralyzing anxiety before significant exams, and the engulfing darkness of depression. I know I'm not alone in these experiences.

My own personal journey:

As an abandoned child, I embarked on a journey that ultimately led me to reconnect with my parents during my teenage years. Through perseverance and resilience, I transformed adversity into my superpower. In school, they teased me about my English, but I became the president of everything, anyway.

Today, I proudly hold four college degrees: a Bachelor's in Arts with a major in Communications, an MBA specializing in Organizational Leadership, a Master's in Science focused on Cyber Security and Counterterrorism, and a Doctorate in Business Administration with a major in International Business.

In September 2023, I am embarking on my fifth academic journey, pursuing a Master's in Science with a specialization in Industrial and Organizational Psychology.

I channel my experiences and knowledge into hosting and producing a livestream and podcast called "Level Up Higher Education Edition." Through this platform, I aim to uplift my community and raise awareness about the multifaceted aspects of human capacity and vulnerability, viewing vulnerability as our superpower.

I firmly advocate for the normalization of acknowledging that it's okay not to be okay and that the pursuit of perfection can be detrimental. My belief in collaboration as the key to success over competition fuels my dedication to making a positive impact on individuals and communities alike.

Additionally, I am proud to share that my reach extends far and wide. My content is available in 25 distribution channels across 6 continents and reaches 73 nations and countries, allowing me to connect with a global audience and spread the message of empowerment and resilience.

The Education System: Balancing tradition with modernity: The challenge for Asian families

I delve into how cultural factors and the education system have significantly shaped my journey as an Asian student. Let's explore the enduring impact of Confucianism, collectivism, and filial piety, the stigma surrounding mental health, and the intricate balance that Asian families strive to maintain.

Confucianism, Collectivism, and Filial Piety: Their Influence on Education

Growing up in an Asian household, the teachings of Confucius weren't just ancient wisdom; they were the guiding principles of life. Respect for authority, emphasis on hierarchy, and the pursuit of knowledge as a noble endeavor were deeply ingrained in my upbringing.

Confucian values profoundly affect education in Asian societies. They emphasize diligence and the pursuit of excellence, a responsibility that often weighs heavily on

Asian students. The desire to honor one's family through academic achievement becomes a formidable burden.

Collectivism, a cultural facet, has left an indelible mark on my educational journey. Belonging to a close-knit community, be it family or cultural group, offers both support and pressure. Expectations from family and the aspiration to make them proud drive academic excellence but also bear a significant emotional burden.

Filial piety, ingrained respect and obedience to parents, is a cornerstone of Asian culture. It compels us to strive for success, often at great personal sacrifice, to fulfill our duties as filial children.

The Stigma of Mental Health in Asian Societies

In Asian societies, mental health has long been veiled in stigma. Discussing anxiety, stress, or depression is often perceived as a sign of weakness. The fear of being labeled as mentally unwell or a burden to one's family can deter us from seeking essential help.

I've felt this stigma firsthand. The reluctance to open up about my struggles, the fear of judgment, and the pressure to project strength have sometimes hindered me from seeking support.

**A Path Forward: Challenging the status quo:
Voices advocating for change**

I share the heartening progress on my journey toward creating a brighter future for Asian students grappling with mental health amidst relentless academic pressures.

Initiatives and Interventions: There's hope in the rising

number of initiatives and interventions supporting Asian students' mental health. From peer support groups to awareness campaigns, these efforts are dismantling the stigma surrounding mental health in our communities. They offer solace and empowerment by acknowledging our shared struggles and offering crucial support.

Challenging the Status Quo: Courageous advocates are challenging the status quo. They're pushing for change by engaging with educational institutions, policymakers, and communities. Their determination reveals that change is possible, even when cultural norms seem entrenched. It's a testament to the power of persistence in creating a more compassionate educational landscape.

Success Stories: Heartwarming success stories abound. Parents are prioritizing their children's well-being over grades, redefining success around happiness and personal growth. Schools and universities are implementing mental health programs, recognizing their role in fostering well-rounded students. And students themselves are becoming advocates, challenging expectations, seeking help, and supporting peers in crisis.

A Path Forward: Reflecting on these efforts, there's a clear path forward—a path marked by compassion, understanding, and a commitment to change. We can expand mental health support, amplify advocates' voices, and draw inspiration from success stories. It won't be without challenges, but it's a path promising a brighter future where Asian students' mental well-being is as valued as their academic achievements.

Nurturing well-rounded individuals: Rethinking success-The role of parents, teachers, and policymakers

In this Journey, We've Uncovered Challenges and Hope

Throughout this journey, we've explored the intricate challenges faced by Asian students in their relentless pursuit of academic excellence.
We've delved into cultural factors, the psychological toll, and the surrounding stigma, all of which intersect in complex ways.

Change is Not Only Possible; It's Essential

I firmly believe that change is not just possible but essential. We possess the power to reshape our educational landscape, redefine success, and foster a more compassionate and balanced environment for Asian students.

Recommendations for Change: Education Reform and Mental Health Support

Education reform stands as a pivotal pillar in this transformation. We must reimagine our educational systems, valuing holistic development alongside academic excellence. Reducing pressure and nurturing an environment where students can thrive without sacrificing their mental well-being is paramount.

The Role of Parents, Teachers, and Policymakers

Parents, as initial educators, hold significant influence. They can encourage open communication, understand their children's needs, and resist undue pressure. Teachers can create inclusive classrooms and offer emotional support, while policymakers can advocate for policies prioritizing mental health in education.

Nurturing Well-Rounded Individuals: Rethinking Success
Success should be redefined to encompass personal growth, resilience, and happiness, not just high grades and prestigious careers.
Our aim should be nurturing well-rounded individuals who navigate life with confidence and empathy.

The Need for Collective Action, Hope for a Balanced Future

As we conclude, let's carry these recommendations for change forward. Let's be advocates for a more compassionate, balanced, and empathetic education system—one where knowledge pursuit harmonizes with students' well-being. Together, we can create a brighter future, free from the relentless pressures of the past.

Urgency, Hope, and Inspiration

As we conclude this chapter of my journey as an Asian American student, the urgency of addressing the mental health struggles that weigh upon us has never been clearer. The time for action is now, and it requires the collective determination of every individual, parent, educator, and policymaker.

Within this pressing need, hope thrives—a hope born from the belief that we have the power to reshape our education system into one where the pursuit of knowledge harmonizes seamlessly with the emotional well-being of our students.

I'm rattled awake with the hope of inspiring you, transcending boundaries, and touching every individual's heart and conscience. We possess the capacity to become champions of change, to champion the cause of mental health, and to cultivate the kind of nurturing environments where students don't just succeed academically; they flourish emotionally, becoming resilient, confident, and empathetic individuals.

In this shared voyage, thank you for being part of this collective journey, where our intertwined experiences ignite the flames of purposeful action and herald transformative change in the lives of our students and the very communities they belong to. Together, we are architects of a brighter, more compassionate future.

I channel my experiences and knowledge into hosting and producing a livestream and podcast called "Level Up Higher Education Edition." Through this platform, I aim to uplift my community and raise awareness about the multifaceted aspects of human capacity and vulnerability, viewing vulnerability as our superpower.

I firmly advocate for the normalization of acknowledging that it's okay not to be okay and that the pursuit of perfection can be detrimental. My belief in collaboration as the key to success over competition fuels my dedication to making a positive impact on individuals and communities alike.

This journey of dedication and sacrifice has been one that has rattled me awake to the power of resilience and the potential we all have to overcome challenges.

Can you relate to a moment in your life that transformed adversity into your own superpower?

Dr. Constance Leyland is on a mission to level up the

world through Education. She is a catalyst for change through collaboration. Tune into her podcast, Level Up where she showcases tales of resilience. Dr. Leyland's Level Up Academy by Docleyland takes her commitment further, providing transformative courses for personal development.

Connect with her here: linkedin.com/in/cjleyland/

THE BIPOLAR PEN ~NICOLE ANGAI-GALINDO

The Bipolar Pen: Unleashing the Gift of a Writer

Every morning I would wake up and pull the rope over my head until it sat comfortably around my neck. Yet it was anything but comfortable wearing the target that hung from it with its fraying ends caused by too many years of use. I'd never considered discarding the target whose bullseye sat right over my heart. Though begrudgingly, I would slip into it as I did my shirt daily.

On a Wednesday a few weeks before Christmas last year, I endured a life-shattering experience - a jarring of the soul caused by the nastiest fall I'd taken in my life. My eyes flew open. At that moment, the stunning realization that I no longer needed to live my life, as I felt society lead me to believe I should, punched me in the head with a Tyson left hook.

As I lay on my back on the hardwood floor in the hallway, just outside of the conference room in our office, I felt the shame of the fall far more than the excruciating heat caused by the pain radiating from the vicinity of my left kneecap. I would later learn that I'd fallen so hard on my left knee, that the echo of my knee hitting the floor was heard by my co-workers. At the time, they were in their offices, separated by the conference room wall and the twenty-four-foot width of the warehouse space.

I slid on my back along the narrow hallway toward the door that offered privacy from the front office. Reaching backward over my head with my left hand, I banged on that door as if my life depended on it. And it did. My left leg was suspended in the air, same as it would have been, had I been doing exercises where I needed to tuck my knees into my chest. I could not straighten my leg.

While I waited for someone to hear me and respond to my urgent banging on the door, I looked at the grotesqueness of the upper half of my kneecap protruding from under my skin. It was lodged in the lower half of my thigh quad.

During the ambulance ride to the hospital, even drugged up on painkillers, I kept thinking, "Now what? How can the mortgage and other bills get paid if I can't work - what if we lose the house? Oh my God, I've only been in this job for five months. I will get fired."

Well, I didn't get fired. What ensued after that accident would catapult my life in a completely different direction... one where getting fired might even be a blessing.

The morning before my major knee surgery, a week after falling, I picked up my cell phone and wrote a post on LinkedIn. The headline of that post, Talk-Thru Thursday, is one I have been sharing on LinkedIn every week since December 15th, 2022. I selfishly created this piece to occupy the extra time I found on my hands; endless amounts of time during the next three months of recovery.

Little did I know that from this selfish act, I would find a community whose support was, and continues to be, more than I've ever experienced from in-person friendships. So began my real life, one with purpose.

I severed the rope that held the target in front of my chest. I no longer allowed my bipolarness to define me as someone who needed to try hard every day, to blend into society by squelching my emotions so much so that during certain times in my life, I wished I weren't here on this earth.

Instead, I used my gift of bipolarness and the time that life had just bestowed upon me, to unleash my buried tumultuous emotions. Much like a painter, who uses their brush in a motion that splatters paint drops onto a canvas, I wielded my fingers, typing every word that sprung from my creative mind, fueled by two minds and two hearts. I owned my story, my bipolar condition, and all the beauty this gift has given me.

What I've discovered, and want to share with the world, is the power of owning your story; of accepting and loving yourself just the way you are. It might seem cliche, but until we can face our reflection in the mirror and embrace all that we see, the good, the bad, and the ugly, we cannot move forward. I remind myself every day that **continuous improvement is better than delayed perfection**.

Start where you are with what you have. You need nothing more. Opening myself up in this way, to myself,

and subsequently putting myself out there on social media, primarily LinkedIn, has benefited me tremendously. In finding others that I can identify with, I can use my voice and my story, to inspire others to open their eyes to their lives. Not to what else is happening around them, but to what is happening *within* them.

Since doing this, one of my greatest passions, writing, is being fulfilled. Emails and the occasional speech for an event hardly scratched the surface of what my capabilities. The more I wrote, the more my writing took on a life of its own. As a result, I opened myself up to opportunities. In doing so, I guested on a live show for Valentine's 2023, which would be the catalyst to starting my own business, The Gifted Bipolar Writer, about four months ago.

My personal growth over these past four months has been astounding. I love myself in a way I never have before. I am confident, take pride in my accomplishments and am inquisitive. Have you ever felt like a nuisance or embarrassed to ask too many questions? Well, don't be. Nowadays I remind myself that to feel temporarily uncomfortable about asking a question is worth it, if I walk away with an answer.

Every day, my self-awareness improves. The more I see about myself, and understand about myself, the more I realize that I have so many admirable qualities.

I feel that people who live with depression but aren't "alive" often allow what others think of them, to become their reality. Accepting their opinion as the confines within which they live their lives.
Someone told me shortly before I started my business that I was crazy if I thought I could break into the world of content creation when it was already so saturated. He scoffed that with ChatGPT, AI, and foreign content creators who could be paid cents on the dollar, why would anyone

pay me to ghostwrite? Today, one of my clients is a recurring $1,000 project. Just yesterday someone reached out to me and wants to meet this week. She is interested in having me write her story. Believe in yourself and your abilities.

Backstage, after that Valentine's Day live show, I met a publisher. I'd not known any publishers before then. She invited me to write a chapter in an anthology called, "Now What?" It was about protecting that sacred space after terrible adversity. I could hardly contain myself. The opportunity of a lifetime, and one that I didn't even know I wanted, fell into my lap. I had one week to hand in that draft. I'd never written outside of my post and blog. I am not a studied writer. I simply said 'yes.' And, with that came the accountability to myself and to the person to whom I'd said yes.

The day before the book launch, another opportunity opened up. Sadly, there was a spat between the publisher and the graphic designer, who ended up pulling her chapter from the book and with it, her graphics to promote the launch. I was on the third week of my 30-day Canva trial. I offered to do the graphics for thirty-nine authors and myself. I left work 15 mins early and stayed up until 2 am the next morning, the day of the launch.

My exhaustion was palpable. Yet, I was flying on a high like nothing I'd ever experienced. Not even after my third ice-cold Corona, with lime and salt, and a deep drag on a cigarette, had I known such an exhilarating feeling.

After that launch, I sealed the deal of a lifetime: to publish a chapter in any of the publisher's upcoming anthologies in trade for the book cover's design. Yes, now I am doing this in addition to the marketing graphics. Another thing I taught myself to do. Remember, there is nothing you can't learn to do. If you are passionate about something, there will always be a burning desire to learn everything there is so you can do it well. Last month, we launched another anthology together. This one, with a book cover I designed, hit #1 International Best Seller within 48 hours. To see my name printed on the inside front cover of the book, as the cover designer, was priceless.

So much more has happened since then, including this anthology you now hold in your hands.

I've created and launched "The Published in Style" package and, my most recent clients were named "#3 Hot New Release" on Amazon this past week. Once again, my book cover design was being showcased for the world to see.

I chose to write a chapter in Rattled Awake to share the moment and consequent events that forced my eyes open. Open to see, and then acknowledge, how every moment I've lived in my past, and every minute I live in this day, is another hour closer to understanding better who I am.

That with every breath I draw and exhale, there is a peaceful ebb and flow of my essence being embraced, and then released into the universe.

Embracing my purpose, fueled by my deep understanding of why, and granting myself the permission to let my passion thrive through my bipolar journey is not just my path to success… it can be yours too!

Nicole Angai-Galindo, aka: "Nic," is on a mission to help others embrace their "bipolarness" as a gift. She is an example to others, having started her own business, The Gifted Bipolar Writer, just after becoming a first-time published author in March, 2023. Today, Nicole is a 2x International Best-Selling Author, and continues to serve her community through her LinkedIn Live audio room NIC – Never In Control and through participation in various uplifting projects such as The 50 Inspiration Connections on LinkedIn. Connect with her on LinkedIn: Nicole (aka "Nic") Angai-Galindo

LIVE YOUR PURPOSE NOW! ~RUSS HEDGE

There's nothing like a life-threatening diagnosis to change your perspective on life. But for me it was so much more: it was having to walk the talk that I had proclaimed for decades. I was being called out by my own disease.

My Rattled Awake story begins here.

"Life is 10% what happens to you and 90% how you react to it." – Charles R. Swindoll

It was July of 2022, and I discovered a concerning spot on the bottom of my foot. I asked my beautiful wife to take a look, and she said, "It looks like a wart." Two months later I was diagnosed with cancer, stage 2A invasive Melanoma.

The "C" word was a bit shocking, but the way the dermatologist described it, it sounded fairly routine. I thought, "No big deal, they will cut out the Melanoma and I'll be all good.

God blessed me with a very positive attitude and perspective on life, so I usually just roll with the punches. *"It's all good"* is my motto!

"Perspective is everything when you are facing challenges in life." - Joni Eareckson Tada

Joni is a quadriplegic, paralyzed from the shoulders down from a diving accident at 17, when she misjudged how shallow the water was in Chesapeake Bay. It is her positive God-given perspective on life that has driven her to do amazing things.

But it is so much easier to have a positive perspective when life is good. It's when the challenges come that the rubber meets the road. It's how you bounce back after you fall down that matters.

> *"It's not how far you fall, but how high you bounce that counts."* -Zig Ziglar

I was referred to Oregon Health Sciences University (OHSU) to see an oncologist surgeon and a plastic surgeon. By the time my appointment arrived, about a month later, they found an additional spot of Melanoma. I was told they would have to remove about half of my instep on my right foot, slide the other half over to cover the weight bearing portion, and borrow skin from another area on my body to finish rebuilding my instep. It was estimated to be a 4–5-hour surgery.

They would also remove a lymph node in my right groin area for testing, just to make sure the cancer hadn't spread. They felt very confident we had caught the cancer early, so the prognosis was good.

I had surgery on November 11th, 2022.

The surgery went well, and they sent me home the next day to begin the slow recovery process. We were all feeling optimistic.
Well, life is full of surprises, and on Thursday, November 17th, I received an unwelcome one.

The day started off great. I went to my post-op appointment at OHSU and was told the cancer removal and the plastic surgery they did to repair my foot was looking good; that I was healing as expected.

After the good news, my beautiful wife, daughter and I drove home and grabbed some Chick-fil-A on the way. I was tired, but feeling great about the doctor's observations.

Then, we got home and I opened my email. I saw an OHSU MyChart Message with the test results from pathology. I was expecting to see positive news.

The first part was great. The bottom of my foot, where they cut out the cancer, looked good. The outer tissue was cancer free. Very. Good. News.

The next part was not so good. In the lymph node they removed in my groin area they found a malignant tumor. My oncology surgeon called a short time later. The way he explained it, that meant the cancer went from Stage 2A, to Stage 3C, very serious, and further treatment or surgery was needed. They were also doing additional tests and scans to make sure it had not gone any further in my body.

The news really shook me and my family. In fact, my son and daughter-in-law called from California to find out the results and as I began to tell them, I looked up at my wife and daughter, both with tears running down their faces. I lost it. I couldn't talk.
Suddenly faced with my own mortality I had to make some decisions. Not just about the cancer, but about how I lived my life, both physically and mentally. Was I taking good care of myself, and a perspective check: What were my real authentic feelings about the whole experience?

I always look for the positive and sometimes overlook what I should be learning from the situation. God was going to use this experience to grow and guide me. I needed to figure out where I was headed now that I had received this unwelcome news.

It was a pivotal moment, and one that took most of the night to recover from. But tomorrow was coming.

My dad, who was my hero, used to always say, *"Tomorrow's a new day!"* He would tell me to try to get a good night's sleep and the morning would bring a fresh perspective.

I truly believe we have to experience our current emotions, but as the saying goes, time heals all wounds, and I knew I was going to grow through this experience and come out better on the other side.

I love the quote by Justin Winski, *"Don't let your circumstances define you. You define your circumstances."*

It is only God and each of us that define who we are and what we are planning to do with our circumstances. We can't just sleepwalk through life. What is our perspective when we are rattled awake?

After the initial shock of the diagnosis, I felt God saying to me, "It is going to be ok. I've got this!" I am a man with a strong faith, and I knew God was not done with me yet. I had a peace about the cancer, but something was still feeling off.

Then God gave me a startling moment of clarity. I realized I had been speaking about a Purpose-Driven Life, but not living one!

I was missing the whole point of my own message.

Was I going to live what I preached?

Was I truly living to Inspire and encourage others with my

own actions, or did I just talk about it?

I believe life happens and then you choose!

It was then that I chose to truly Live Life On Purpose and With My Purpose. My 'Why?' or purpose, came alive: I am here to *inspire and encourage others to live a purpose-driven life of significance*. To help them make a difference *now*! To make an impact for good, *now*!

And suddenly God had me in my own workshop, learning the lesson I had taught and talked about so many times.

I had a choice to make and suddenly realized the reality that it was so much easier said than done.

It was time to stop the talking and start the walking!

Winston Churchill said *"It's not enough to have lived. We should be determined to live for something."*
In 2020, at the height of Covid, I wrote and released my first book, "Befuddled? Live the Life You Choose!" It was a book about living with purpose and a positive mindset, in spite of life's circumstances. I talked about perspective and how you look at life… especially through life's challenging circumstances.

I have had some momentous things happen over my life. In my book, I wrote about my near fatal car accident in July of 1983; I was only 19 years old.

I've lost both my parents: my dad to lung cancer and my Mama to Alzheimer's. All of these have happened in the month of July - coincidentally the same month I found what we thought was a wart on the bottom of my foot.

I am planning to skip July from here on out!

I went through a major change in 2020, going from my corporate job as Sales and Marketing Manager to starting my own business. What started out as a real challenge, especially during Covid, turned out to be one of the best things that ever happened to me.

So, even though I lived through challenges, this was different. This really rattled me awake and shook me to the core. A life-threatening, unbelievable disease was actually happening to me.

I had to suddenly be present… in the NOW. I told myself, in spite of what's happening, today is my day! Today is an opportunity and I choose to live my purpose.

It was time to start encouraging and inspiring others. Not just caring, but sharing. I took a moment to be vulnerable and I started sharing my story on social media. As my friend Nancy Debra Barrows would say, it was time to start #RadiatingReal.

As I shared, I realized the impact on others. I felt God using me to share with others that I was living my journey while keeping a positive perspective. I was honest and vulnerable and shared how, although it was not easy, I was moving forward in spite of the ongoing challenges.

Truth is, they didn't stop coming. After the first round of Immunotherapy, they found more cancer in the lymph nodes in my right groin. I had to choose to change drugs in my treatment, or surgery. After a weekend of prayer, I chose treatment.

Unfortunately, my body didn't react well to the treatment. I got extremely sick, and then contracted Type 1 Diabetes as my pancreas began to shut down.

I continued to be vulnerable and share, and it kept coming.

I had to have another surgery to remove more cancer. It was an invasive surgery and they removed 11 lymph nodes in my upper right groin area, as well as moving a muscle to protect that area.

Once again, a long recovery, but this time with a great result.

About a week and a half after the surgery, the pathology results came back and they found cancer only in one of the inflamed lymph nodes; it was contained. They had removed all the cancer.
They had planned to do radiation after the surgery, but the OHSU Tumor Board met, reviewed my situation and decided no more treatment was needed because I was cancer-free.

I continue to share my journey and reach out to those in need, where possible. My story is ongoing, and I intend to keep encouraging and inspiring others through my actions.

Our story never ends, and the perspective we embrace will make a significant difference.

Do you need to be Rattled Awake?

Is today the day you decide to live your true, authentic purpose-driven life?

Russ Hedge is on a mission to Inspire and Encourage others to live their Best Life Now. He wants to help them be World Changers, Difference Makers, and use their God-Given Gifts to do Amazing Things! Known as an "Inspiration Specialist," he is a Marketing Coach, Keynote Speaker, Podcaster, Livestream

Producer and Author of "Befuddled? Live the Life You Choose!" He has been married to Leah for over 35 years, has two adult children, Kyla and Connor, and a daughter-in-law, Gabby. His goal is to add value to people by encouraging and helping them live a more engaged and positive life.

Connect with Russ at russ@russhedge.com.

GROWING WITH THE FLOW ~WILLIE J.

It was bad enough losing my mother as a young man, but when I lost two extremely close family members in a year's time, I was really pressed to celebrate my faith and rejoice rather than to mourn over their loss. After all they were no longer suffering here and were finally resting peacefully in the Creator's bosom. I'm talking about no more crying, no more dying, no more hurting, and no more dealing with the cares of this unpredictable world.

Over a period of time, I'd learned to leverage my pains and turn them into my greatest gains, like building an award-winning entertainment company right from the ground up, and having my work rising continuously to #1 Top Spots. It reminds me of a great quote by the legendary Kobe Bryant who stated:

> *"Everything negative - pressure, challenges -*
> *is all an opportunity for me to rise."*

Every adversity, every challenge, is an opportunity for me to ascend higher. As bad as I needed the sunshine in my life, I would also realize the need to have the raindrops falling as well. I actually needed this rain in order to mature, progress and GROW up further into my overall purpose. I like to call it my GROWING PAINS, including the pain of once facing up to 30 years in a maximum penitentiary, with a beautiful daughter on the way; the pain of losing my 13-year-old best friend to gun violence... he was simply skipping class and he got shot!?? And that pain felt from witnessing a young man shot in the face, killed in his own backyard, while I was throwing the football with my cousin.

I have always been "Rattled Awake" in some way or another. Can you relate? I'm certain that you can. Life can be like a multitude of unexpected waves streaming continuously down our peaceful shores. As the big waves begin to GROW bigger and taller, so does the unpredictable PRESSURE.

When I take the 'URE' off of this word PRESSURE, I am left with the word PRESS. So, when the PRESSURE comes, it actually becomes my opportunity to PRESS forward and grow harder.

Now you may be asking yourself, "Where did he discover such an amazing revelation? Or, how did he come up with such a gem of a masterpiece?"

Well, I am so very glad that you asked!

It was only a few years ago when I had been scheduled to record my first international hit record entitled, "Sunshine with The Rain," featuring my client, Arthur Flash Johnson. But just a few days ahead of recording it, I woke up sick; vomiting intensely over the toilet. I'm talkin' *very* intense hours of suffering here. Meanwhile, I got a strange call that my cousin Lamar had been found dead in the backseat of his car. Needless to say, this would change the whole trajectory of my recording session, just days away.

Boy, was I devastated by this sudden tragedy. I mean sure, I could've taken the easy way out by cancelling the session. But with the help of God, I chose to be strong and LEVERAGE my high PRESSURE into something very special. I can remember clearly telling my engineers, Ken and Arthur, "Let's keep the session rolling forward. Something extraordinary will happen as a result of it." Well, that is exactly what happened. The song was picked up by the legendary "Lynyrd Skynyrd" member,

Stephen Wrench, co-writer of the hit record "Sweet Home Alabama." Stephen immediately got behind the record, pushing it overseas onto the Top 200 European International Music Charts. Let's just say that I am delighted I decided to "GROW WITH THE FLOW," rather than go against it.

Now, we were on the move, and it was finally time to record my next charity-based hit single entitled, "We Love You Puerto Rico" featuring various artists. It was an historic composition I had written on behalf of all of the Hurricane Maria victims. This song was scheduled to be the first official release through my company, Pure Mission Entertainment. But before I could even get on the plane to leave and actually finalize the recording, I would get a very disturbing phone call about my Aunt and a cousin who had suddenly passed away, just one day apart. I couldn't believe it, I was like "Wow! Here we go again." The timing couldn't have been any worse.

So, I finally got on the plane to Los Angeles, California, to record my new hit single. Before I could even land properly, I would receive yet another set of disturbing phone calls. My three good friends had all been involved in multiple freak accidents simultaneously. One had been nearly killed in a brutal head-on collision, another was shot in the head, and another was rushed to the hospital due to a bad sugar-diabetic attack. Talk about being "Rattled Awake" and "Growing with the Flow."

Fortunately, the good news is that they all recovered well and survived. Even better, this charity-based hit record went on to be a bigger smash than the last one. It placed even higher on the Top 200 European International Music Charts. The record received an amazing write–up article from the legendary Broadway World via New York, bringing in millions of streams in 184+ countries, along with a massive amount of proceeds and donations sent worldwide. Eventually, the official music video made its debut as well on ABC30 TV and KCTV5 via Better Kansas City. I'm talking about right during the heart of the pandemic aka COVID-19.

Now obviously we were told to be extremely careful about going live and direct with the people at major TV networks, primarily because so many people had died and more were dropping like flies everyday. I'm sure that you can relate in some painful way or another. My business partner, Aaron, and I, chose to prayerfully GROW WITH THE FLOW, to hit the road with unwavering courage and complete fearlessness. I am grateful to God for safeguarding us on this tedious journey every step of the way.

We were still riding high when I would be asked to write and record yet another charity-based record through my company. This song featured artist and best friend, Terry Sanford, on the background vocals. It was a dedication song to all of the COVID-19 victims near and far.

I can remember traveling home on one beautiful day from Richmond, Virginia, wrapping up a major front cover shoot. Me and some of my staff members had just finished celebrating in Virginia Beach. Before I could even arrive back home, I got a devastating call saying that Terry was unresponsive and was in intensive care. Boy, was I Rattled Awake and crushed, to say the very least. I thought that we both had plenty of time together in this entertainment industry. But before we could actually release the song, Terry suddenly passed away from a very serious illness.

We finally released the COVID anthem and let's just say that it became another big smash very quickly, accumulating over 10 million streams worldwide with global donations, along with the music video also making its debut on

ABC30TV with an amazing interview. Then the rest, as they would say, is history!

My unwavering commitment to "GROW WITH THE FLOW" remains resolute and regardless of the many challenges that come my way. I eagerly anticipate the opportunity to cultivate more hope for those in need through the avenues of music, art, public speaking, literature, coaching, and global outreach.

Our journey in life is a testament to our ability to adapt, evolve, and make a positive impact on the world around us. As we continue down this path, let us remember that each step forward holds the potential to inspire, uplift, and create a brighter future for all. Thank you for joining me on this journey of growth and hope. Together, we can continue to make a meaningful difference in the lives of others and in the world we all share.

Willie J. is on a mission to empower more people and change more lives while creating more hope through arts, business, coaching and entertainment. As a world-renowned entrepreneur, author, artist, speaker and coach of the John Maxwell Team, this St. Louis native has been featured as a Top Entrepreneur in both Forbes and GQ Magazine. His company, Pure Mission Entertainment, hit #1 in the top 10 spots of NY Weekly, LA Weekly, LA Wire, and US Reporter, to name just a few outstanding accolades. Most recently he graced the front cover of the "Los Angeles Magazine" with an article that can be read on his company website: puremissionent.com.

THE PRESSURE COOKER ~LONNEE REY

"This stupid pressure canner is just in the way," I mumbled. I should have rolled up my sleeves, but instead, held it at arm's length like it had cooties, relocating it for the fifth time - this time, I hid it under a blanket. Out of sight out of mind, right? It was a scary behemoth of a machine that I'd heard all sorts of nightmare stories about. HSSSST! It was the canner, haunting me in my dreams.

I was like, "It's gonna blow up on me. I will do it wrong, and the jars will explode inside." I wondered why it did not come complete with safety goggles, that's how scared I was of it. It's amazing I ever became a chef, considering how afraid I am of lighting a gas stove or oven. I always got someone else to do it. The same thing happened in culinary school: an accident left me unable to taste a lot of food. I had to have another person season my sauces and soups. In spite of that, I was awarded the "Most Outstanding Freshman of the Year" scholarship. Further proof that, with determination, we can overcome a lot of things.

Where was my can-do attitude about the canner??

"Come on, get over it. You've been through worse things," I thought. They say people most fear death and public speaking. Age 12, I had a near-death experience; and I found that public speaking is easier than small talk at a party. These chart-topping fears aren't nearly as bad as we imagine them to be. Been there, done that.

I'm sure we can all relate to something we should have faced sooner than later, and when we finally did, it turned out okay. As they say, everything you want is on the other side of fear. You probably hear this a lot, too: What is your 'why'? Why are you motivated to do something? Let that motivation pull you through to the other side. There has to be some sort of reward, or avoidance of a negative outcome, to get you through it. I certainly had that in spades.

It all started when I ran into some alarming headlines on alternative news platforms. The terrible decimation of crops that are not going to come back, and the loss of nearly two thousand food processing plants, coincidentally all due to fire, led to my permanently raised eyebrow. What the heck was going on?? As far as food went, the writing was on the wall. It wasn't just some crazy preppers being hoarders of food for a pending Armageddon. This was real and it was happening right under our noses. The bigger alarm was that few people knew about this. With all the crazy things happening in our world, I wanted to make sure that at least one thing in my life would be secure.

I like to eat. I'm thinking, it's a good idea. I'm really not trying to fast. I know they recommend it, but I'm not really trying to do that right now, or in the future. The news I read was disturbing enough. It's hard to do anything when we are not at peace. What's also true is that we can think better when we're not hungry. We hear about inflation or other things like that lately. All of these things want to steal our peace. If you know it's going to rain, grab an umbrella.

"Don't be scared, be prepared," was the motto of cooking and preparedness-oriented YouTubers. Well, that much made sense, especially after watching people panic-buying pallets of water and fighting over the last four-pack of toilet paper.

That pressure canner and I had been in a standoff for a year. What was another week? I researched YouTube channels for recipes and regulations on using a pressure canner. I found another way to procrastinate, writing a tongue-in-cheek email to Presto canner, suggesting they consider including safety glasses and a DVD coaching program to talk us 'Chicken Little' types down off the ledge. I imagined a soothing voice coaxing flocks of new canners back into the kitchen. *Cluck! Cluck!*

I must sound wildly disturbed to you at this point, but I'm okay with that…I hear it's endearing to see someone's authentic knee-quivering moments in life. How we doin'? Moving on…

In my research, I found a frequently used hashtag: #shtf. It means, (when) Shit Hits The Fan. Oh, OK. Wait, what are they talking about? Have you ever heard that before? It was a new term to me. I spoke to the computer screen as if it would answer, 'Well, what are you guys actually expecting? Like, what does #shtf mean? Is it that bombs will be dropping and everything's fine till then?' I wasn't really sure what to make of that bit, and the computer screen was silent.

I learned a #shtf moment wasn't a cataclysm. It wasn't Armageddon. All of us have #shtf moments in our lives. I began to see how it applied now in my life. I began to understand: you need to take care of this because prices aren't going down, and availability may change. I'd already seen how tentative the supply chain was when the local grocery store was out of navy beans and powdered milk for at least six months.

Then, a personal #shtf happened: A terrible fall that left me with a broken wrist and a sprained arm from fingertips to elbow. Overnight, I became a one-handed Wanda. As I write this, the leeks and potatoes I bought the day before the accident are still in the refrigerator, waiting to become soup. I can't peel or cut round vegetables. Try to butter a piece of toast with one hand. What a joke! I learned how to wedge jars with my hip against the counter, and use my good hand to open them. However, attempts to use a rubber band to hold the handle of my hand can opener resulted in tears of frustration and a phone call, "Hey, neighbor, would you please open this can of fruit cocktail for me?" A very thoughtful friend surprised me with the gift of an electric can opener. Normally that is a two-handed operation, as well. But, where there is a will, there's a way. Pushing the can opener against the wall as a brace, and after three or four attempts, it worked. If only it was so easy to brace, and butter, a slice of toast.

I thank God for the forethought of canning and the courage to embrace it...it has literally saved my can. I could not drive myself to the grocery store for six weeks following the accident. Thank goodness I had enough prepared so that even a one-handed Wanda could continue to have three squares a day.

This mantra, "I AM divinely guided, connected, and protected," is something I wanted to share with you. It helps to remind yourself – to repeat it often – especially when uncertainty sets in. I think we are all divinely guided, connected, and protected, frankly. Divine guidance is like intuition, and I've never met a person who regretted following their intuition.

It works out really well when we listen to the still small

voice inside; the one that nudges and guides us like an inner GPS. I call it "the BIG Yes." By definition, "the BIG Yes" can look crazy to other people, defy logic to the casual observer and yet, it's still a good idea. You are the authority over your life. Who cares what other people think? What calls to you is for *you.*

I believe I was led to the news about food supply issues, so, I put on my big girl panties and apologized to the pressure canner for all the glaring looks. The year-long standoff had finally come to an end. I felt silly. What was I so worried about? Ohh yeah: I was listening to other people, giving them power over my actions. You see, the people who had good experiences were not the ones telling stories; it was the ones who didn't know what they were doing that got the most attention. Duly noted.

Like learning to ride a bicycle, then getting so good you did it with no hands, I got cocky with the whole canning thing. I experimented; started combining stuff that just didn't belong in a jar together. Not everything was a good idea, but the point is that what at first was so scary really wasn't so bad. I had wonderful tasting soups stocked up, and retired the canner, for now. It gives me peace of mind to know that it's there.

I've since learned that the Amish have been doing water bath canning, which does not involve a gigantic metal pressure canner, and their results are the same; have been for ions. Unfortunately, at first, I believed the hype that it was not okay to waterbath can most foods. Well, that didn't exactly turn out to be true. I wish I had known. I probably would have had a lot more inventory to fall back on in this current #shtf situation.

Prior to the accident, and with solid research tucked under

my arm, I was excited to tell my neighbors the news. Surely, they wanted to have food security too, right? "Make sure you stock up for yourselves and your pets because this stuff isn't on the news. Don't be scared, be prepared," I said.

Condescending smiles, 'deer in the headlights' looks, along with some very obvious and wide berths given since then, have shown me apathy on a whole new level. They simply do not care. Put the gun away, don't shoot the messenger! Everyone has opinions, but these are facts. The number of food processing plants being torched has only continued to grow in number, but I gave up trying to say anything to them.

There's a Zen expression, "it's not a gift unless the receiver wants it" which helps to keep in mind when your great idea, or intentions, are kicked to the curb. Maybe they don't want to take a look at it, I don't know. I would think you'd want to keep eating. Regardless, I just had to say to myself, "Ohhh, okay, it's like that, huh? OH, OK."

The upside of their apathy is that it prompted a deep look into personality traits; an analysis as to who would, or would not "be there" if ever there came a future #shtf moment. I took mental notes on behavior and recognized some telltale signs that help when it comes to discerning who would be great to have in a foxhole, and who would not.

I use "OH, OK" a lot these days. It has become a habit; a quiet and handy response tactic to the insanity seen on the global stage. NO, it is not okay that we are faced with a statistical impossibility and 'coincidental' loss of our food manufacturing. Who is doing this? I have no idea. It doesn't matter. *Delete the need to understand.* Somebody is up to no good, and it's up to us to be prepared, not scared.

I saw people listening to sources and resources that really weren't that, ummm...informed. They were making decisions based on half the story. If you only hear half the story, what's the other half? I was doing my part to ring the proverbial triangle on the porch. I think it was an unwelcome noise. Cue shoulder shrug. All of these events and reactions from other people, including my own, have been teaching moments for sure.

As a result of these rattled awake moments, I ended up writing a book called "How to Deal with a Dumbass: what to do and say when they head your way." It's like a field guide to potholes and the people who dig them. It is intentionally funny and authentic as the day is long because *yours truly* has been gullible, full of wishful thinking and misguided hope that if I looked hard enough, or stuck around long enough, the good would outweigh the bad. Not everybody qualifies for the foxhole, but God-knows I kept trying. There is a high price paid for wearing rose-colored glasses.

Discernment is practically a survival skill – and one we all need to make choices in our favor. It isn't selfish, it's essential. We live in crazy times. Who we surround ourselves with matters now more than ever. Ensuring that you have people who have your back in a pinch is of utmost importance.

Protect your peace at all costs.

These rattled awake moments have become a mission to encourage sovereignty, and a movement fueled through collective passions to "Say it forward" via the Rattled Awake anthology series. The need for discernment, along with strategies to spot trouble *before* it becomes your problem, have become a book and hilarious podcast, *How to Deal with a Dumbass (a spiritual perspective).* "Your contagious laugh always makes me feel better, Lonnee."

A man in his late 50s wrote me a note to say that my Dumbass book helped him escape a dangerous cult in Norway. It feels good to know that something so simple as sharing embarrassing stories ('cuz I have been a duhmmy many times in life), is changing lives.

You never know what impact you will have, do you? Taking action is only way to move forward.

What can you do to steady and ready yourself come what may?

One final thought:

When you wear rose-colored glasses, you miss the red flags. So, as hard as it is to take them off, it's worth it. You will be glad you did.

Go tell that mean old pressure canner in your life that it doesn't scare you anymore. Follow your "Big Yes." You will be glad you did. When your #shtf moment comes and rattles you awake, you will already be prepared to get through it.

Lonnee Rey is on a mission to broadcast the voices of people whose stories will elevate, inspire and change our world for the better. She is a story development editor, concierge book producer, multi-show podcast host and authors' promotional messaging advisor. You can find "Life Lessons Learned from a Lousy Mother" and her "Dumbass" book on Amazon; her podcast is on Spotify.

If you would like to share your Rattled Awake moment, connect with her via linkedin.com/in/lonnee/.

IT'S ALL AN ILLUSION
~STEVE KIDD

"This is ridiculous," I said to myself with a laugh. "I'm sure by now. Security cameras and probably all the employees here at this grocery store think I'm insane."

I sat there. Laughing at myself. "Go ahead", I thought, "At least this time I wasn't in tears."

I was totally lost. I had been to this grocery store a thousand times. Shopped for food for so many years. I was stuck. I couldn't do anything. I didn't even know where to begin.

"Happy birthday to me," I said to myself. Fearing that the laughter was going to give way to sorrow. It was my birthday. A day to celebrate. I had this amazing opportunity to be able to for the first time, maybe ever, something I had never done. I had the chance to do only and exactly what I wanted.

But what did I want?

I didn't know.

At the time I didn't realize how grateful and how lucky I was to be able to go round and round and round a grocery store. To pick something out, put it back, decide what you want, change your mind, and do that over and over again. It didn't matter whether it took you a minute or hours. It was something that I had always taken for granted. Oh sure, there were things in life that I had to keep to a schedule and couldn't just wander aimlessly in the store because I had places to go and things to do, BUT. If I wanted to, when I had the time, it was an option. I couldn't just spend all day every day in grocery stores. It didn't matter.

Then the world turned.

From that day laughing, holding back tears, and trying to figure out a whole new life; and 'what did it mean to truly celebrate me?' to just a few months later, where the whole world changed. Within days the bottom had dropped out in the world. Not only were you supposed to not go into Grocery stores, but when you had to, you had to wear a mask. When you had to go there were people looking at you all the time assuming you were diseased. Assuming you were going to either be the next person who died, or the person that got them sick.

You see the part of that story that I haven't told you yet Is that I was in one of those scooters driving around the store. That's right one of those little carts with the basket in the front in the grocery store because my physical health wasn't good enough to walk that much. So now when I went into the store, people assumed I was one of those "High risk" people and they avoided me like I was the plague. There was after all a pandemic. The whole world was going to die and it was all sickos like me that were just the worst.

We all KNEW this was our last breath. I mean turn on any TV station, and they would confirm that as well as tell you how many people have died today, this week, this month. Every station would tell you that right this very moment you were going to die. You just knew that everybody in the whole world was actually dying and there was nothing you could do about... Well except never leave your house ever again.

That's what they wanted us to think.

It made this simple process of just going to the grocery store a whole different world from that day not that many days ago.

I had an awakening on my birthday. Though the time in the store, and worse the day I drove around for 2 hours literally unable to decide for myself what I wanted to have for lunch, had helped me realize that I needed to learn to love me. I had never really done that. I never had really required it of anybody else, and I most definitely had never required it of myself. I had taken up the work and really began to work on learning to take care of myself.

Then the whole world conspired against me to tell me to stay home, don't take care of yourself, don't go out, don't exercise, don't breathe on anybody, and whatever you do, sit in front of the TV all day and wait to die.

Remember those days?

About 3 weeks into the covid lockdown, I remember being in the grocery store, again looking at the shelf wondering if I had enough toilet paper at home or if I was going to settle for the rough one-ply. I had been warned that as the poster child for contributing factors that I was, I needed to buy enough food to last me for potentially a month, or perhaps the rest of my life. We had come through 15 days to slow the curve and had decided that we needed another 30. They were encouraging us to double down, to go out even less, to do even less, to be around no one, to implode.

How was I going to grow? How was I going to learn to love myself and develop healthy boundaries with other people? How could I learn to require more of them? How could I learn it was ok to not diminish myself in order to make other people feel okay? How could I learn any of this when now I couldn't even be with anybody? How was I gonna do that?

As I created a grocery list on the fly in my head, putting together meals several weeks in advance. Trying to figure out what would fit into my little refrigerator and freezer. What things could be stored on the shelf and would stay stable potentially for a long time? What if this was even longer than the 30 days they were saying now?

Once again in the store, I laughed. I had an epiphany. Something I'd love to share with you. You see. It's all an illusion. Everything that we take for granted today is only one breath away from being taken away from us forever. This doesn't mean we have to be militant and march in the streets, though some do. This doesn't mean that we need to take to the internet and start a revolution amongst everybody we know. But it does mean we need to be aware just how precious each day is. We need to respect and love ourselves.

You see, as the Bible says, "What was intended for evil, God used for good." He allowed me a sanctuary to be hidden from the world. I mean after all, that's what we were supposed to do and all we pretty much could do. So, during that time, I studied, I learned, I grew, and I fell in love with a person that, for the most part, I didn't even know. I learned how to love…me. I learned to begin to see all of the things that people had complimented me on that I couldn't hear. I began to learn how to say 'thank you' when someone complimented me. I began to see that everyone's story, and everyone's voice, mattered.

By that time, I had already worked with thousands upon thousands of authors, helping them share their story. I was good at emphasizing them. Even though I had had all of that success...nobody knew. Even though I literally created a concept used by seemingly everyone now to become a best-selling author, nobody knew it was me that created the formula used by so many to do that. Nobody even knew who I was. But I knew...I truly knew that in my small way, I was present in every single author's story. I knew deep inside that it was me, quietly shining my light and changing lives for the better.

And so, while the world was tucked away, I allowed the rattling in my soul to wake me up. I came to life. I shined my light to anyone who got near me. Sending out love and light and life to them. And helping them know that they can share their story too. That today matters. That it's not about getting to somewhere where things are going to be perfect, but rather it's about taking our win for today. It's about taking the lessons we've learned from the losses of yesterday, growing ourselves, and also helping others find their rattled awake moment. It's about showing someone also how to learn to live, love themselves,

Be free, and make the difference in the world that only they could make. It's about learning to maximize the time that is today. Because today is the only day we know that we have.

Steve Kidd is on a mission to help 1 million people uplevel by sharing their lives and their message with the world. Steve would love to help share you with the world. To connect with Steve, go to ThrivingBestSellers.com

AN OPEN INVITATION

You are invited to share your perspective-altering story in an upcoming volume of the "Rattled Awake" series. *Please do* - there are people waiting to be moved into action by your courage, resiliency and positive outlook.

How have you been affected over the past five years? Did you suffer a lay-off and become an entrepreneur? Perhaps, you realized you deserved to be treated better, and left an abusive relationship? As a parent, did you see the need to remove your child from public school and take on the task of home-schooling? Were your spiritual gifts awakened, and you embraced them, no matter what other people had to say about it?

In what ways were you motivated to take back authority over your own life? Were you compelled to take action after seeing the truth about a particular issue, person or regulation that simply did not seem right?

What happened, what did you do, and who have you become, as a result?

> *"Don't let the music die with you."*
> -Dr. Wayne Dyer

Please contact one of the co-authors or
visit www.OfficialRattledAwake.com for details